Biomes on Planet Earth

GRASSLAND BIOME

Kerri Mazzarella

Table of Contents

A Starfish Book

SEAHORSE PUBLISHING

Teaching Tips for Caregivers:

As a caregiver, you can help your child succeed in school by giving them a strong foundation in language and literacy skills and a desire to learn to read.

This book helps children grow by letting them practice reading skills.

Reading for pleasure and interest will help your child to develop reading skills and will give your child the opportunity to practice these skills in meaningful ways.

- Encourage your child to read on her own at home
- Encourage your child to practice reading aloud
- Encourage activities that require reading
- Establish a reading time
- Talk with your child
- Give your child writing materials

Teaching Tips for Teachers:

Research shows that one of the best ways for students to learn a new topic is to read about it.

Before Reading

- Read the "Words to Know" and discuss the meaning of each word.
- Read the back cover to see what the book is about.

During Reading

- When a student gets to a word that is unknown, ask them to look at the rest of the sentence to find clues to help with the meaning of the unknown word.
- Ask the student to write down any pages of the book that were confusing to them.

After Reading

- Discuss the main idea of the book.
- Ask students to give one detail that they learned in the book by showing a text dependent answer from the book.

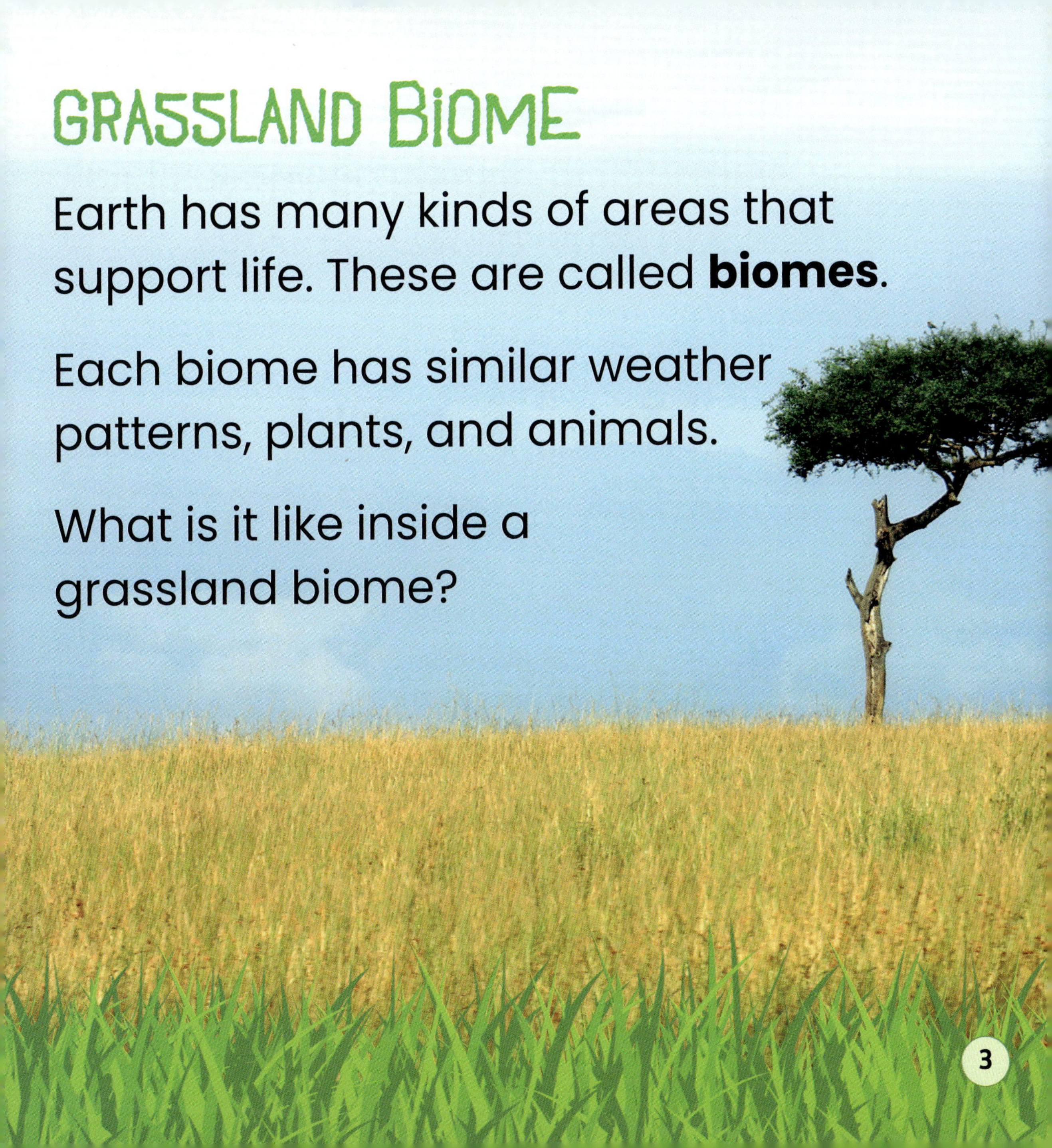

GRASSLAND BIOME

Earth has many kinds of areas that support life. These are called **biomes**.

Each biome has similar weather patterns, plants, and animals.

What is it like inside a grassland biome?

Grasslands are large, open areas with low-growing plants.

About one **quarter** of Earth's land is grassland.

DID YOU KNOW?

The Northern Great Plains is one of the world's largest grasslands. It is found in the northern United States and Canada.

Grasslands get more rain than deserts.

They do not get enough rain for forests to grow.

They are hot in the summer and cold in the winter.

DID YOU KNOW?

During rainy times, colorful wildflowers bloom.

Grasslands in different parts of the world have different names.

They might be called **prairies**, **steppes**, or **savannas**.

DID YOU KNOW?

Wild horses live on steppes in Asia.

People use grasslands for farms and ranches.

Corn, wheat, and other crops grow in the rich soil.

Cattle **graze** on the grass.

Grasslands are full of life.

Thousands of kinds of grass grow.

They feed many animals.

Their deep roots keep soil from washing away.

DID YOU KNOW?

Pronghorns hide their babies in tall grass to keep them safe.

Prairie dogs loosen and **fertilize** the soil.

Many animals live in the tunnels they dig.

DID YOU KNOW?

Huge areas of connected tunnels are called prairie dog towns.

Elephants flatten tall grass, making room for small animals.

Their poop spreads seeds across the grassland.

All living things in the grassland biome work together for survival.

The grassland biome is important for our planet.

How will you help protect it?

Words to Know

biomes (BYE-ohmz): large areas of similar ecosystems that share weather patterns, rainfall amounts, and types of plants and animals

fertilize (FUR-tuh-lize): to put nutrients and other materials into soil to make it richer so that plants grow better

graze (graze): to feed on grass growing in a field

prairies (PRAIR-eez): large areas of flat or rolling grassland with few or no trees, especially in North America

quarter (KWOR-tur): one of four equal parts

savannas (suh-VAN-uh): flat, grassy plains with few or no trees found in tropical areas, especially Africa

steppes (steps): wide treeless plains found in Asia and parts of Europe

Index

Comprehension Questions

1. Grasslands get more rain than
- a. prairies.
- b. deserts.
- c. farms.

2. People use grasslands for
- a. digging tunnels.
- b. growing trees.
- c. farming.

3. Elephants spread _____ through grasslands.
- a. small animals
- b. seeds
- c. rain

4. **True or false:** A prairie is not a grassland.

5. **True or false:** Grasses can have deep roots.

Answers
1. b 2. c 3. b 4. False 5. True

About the Author

Kerri Mazzarella was born in New Hampshire and raised in South Florida. She graduated college from Florida State University. After college she worked in the school system as a Speech Language Pathologist. She has a love for children and is passionate about literacy and learning. She lives in South Florida with her husband, Chris. She has four children, and two dogs. They enjoy family time outside and love to travel.

Written by: Kerri Mazzarella
Design by: Kathy Walsh
Editor: Kim Thompson

Library of Congress PCN Data
Grassland Biome / Kerri Mazzarella
Biomes on Planet Earth
ISBN 978-1-63897-467-3 (hard cover)
ISBN 978-1-63897-582-3 (paperback)
ISBN 978-1-63897-697-4 (EPUB)
ISBN 978-1-63897-812-1 (eBook)
Library of Congress Control Number: 2021953373

Printed in the United States of America.

Seahorse Publishing Company
www.seahorsepub.com

Published in the United States
Seahorse Publishing
PO Box 771325
Coral Springs, FL 33077

Photographs/Shutterstock: Cover & TOC: ©A-Star, ©Jane Rix, ©Mironov Konstantin, ©ANTSTUDIO; Pg 3-21 ©Mironov Konstantin; Pg 6, 7, 9, 13, 15: ©GraphicStore; Pg 3: ©drasa; Pg 4: ©turtix; Pg 6: ©Nancy Bauer; Pg 8: ©isarescheewin; Pg 10: ©Yuriy Kulik; Pg 11: ©symbiot; Pg 12: ©Floki; Pg 13: ©Elijah Knecht, ©Michelle Holihan; Pg 14: ©Nagel Photography; Pg 15: ©Zoltan Tarlacz; Pg 16: ©Sergi Ferrete on Unsplash; Pg 17: ©Henry Wrenn; Pg 18: ©Jane Rix; Pg 20: ©Olexandr Panchenko

SEAHORSE PUBLISHING